INDEX

	Page
The Cook	3
The Crawfish	4
Things to Know	5
The Roux	6
The Boil	9
The Gumbo	9
The Bisque	10
The Ettouffee	12
The Jambalaya	13
The Courtbouillion	13
Stuffed Egg Plant	14
The Okra Casserole	15
Smothered	15
The Centerfold	16
Stuffed Crawfish	18
Fried Crawfish	18
The Piquante	19
The Stew	20
The Supreme	21
The Salad	21
Egg Plant Casserole	22
Stuffed Bell Pepper	23
Hors D'oeuvres	24
The Pie	24
Bienville	25
Deviled	26
The Soup	26
The Fondue	27
Congealed Salad	28
The Creole	29
Mushroom Casserole	29
The Amandine	30
The Cajun	31

Copyright 1982
by
Cajun Country Cookbook, Inc.
P.O. Box 1687
Opelousas, Louisiana 70570

CALL OUR TOLL FREE NUMBER:
1-800-551-9066
LOUISIANA RESIDENTS CALL:
1-318-948-4691

Edited by
Slyvia Jane Barbre

Illustrations by
Cyril J. Forest

A Souvenir of the Cajun Country

To _____

From _____

ISBN: 0-9604580-0-X

THE COOK

Please permit me to introduce myself, although I'm sure it's quite unnecessary, for who does not already know the name of Dalmatian Dominic Dupre or the 320 lb. 5 foot 4 inch frame, the heavy mustache and eyebrows of the world famous Dupre. I am occasionally mistaken for that other world famous person, the detective Frank Cannon, but I'm sure he is often mistaken for Dupre.

It is by one's work, by one's creations that there can be no mistake in recognition. Who, when experiencing an elegant bisque or when tasting an exquisite etouffee does not say "This must be the work of Dupre"? YES, my friends, I am that same Dupre, Known to the finest restaurants of the world — The Purple Palace Cafe of Mamou, Lafleur's Restaurant & Truck Stop between Krotz Springs and Baton Rouge, Mom's Cafe & Pancake House of Breaux Bridge, even in Shreveport they know Dupre. Ahh yes, all over the world.

It is Dupre, who has brought the crawfish out of the mud to it's present heights and glory. It is with the Jambalia, the etouffee, and the bisque that Dupre has lifted the crawfish to the high esteem of the gourmet's table. I ask you, where would the crawfish be without Dupre. On the other hand where would Dupre be without the crawfish? For the maestro to give credit to the fiddle is a magnificent gesture. No? But enough of me, to say more would be immodest. Let us rather, turn to my indomitable little friend, THE CRAWFISH.

THE CRAWFISH

It is with great honor and pleasure that I introduce the crawfish. That seemingly insignificant little crustacean that lives below the earth for five months of the year then comes out to infest the bayous and rice fields with their succulent little bodies. Little, yes. Insignificant, NO. For what better friend can a man have?

He is fearless as a lion and loyal as a dog. With the heart greater than the lion he will stand against any foe. I once saw one stand his ground and defend his home against a bull-dozer many times his size. With claws outstretched and snapping he fought to the last. Valiantly, he gave his life in defense of his home.

With tears welling in my eyes I picked up his broken little body and vowed I would never again operate a bulldozer.

I once kept one as a pet. Not only was he affectionate, loyal and easy to keep but also came in handy one night when I came up short for a recipe.

The loyalty of the crawfish is un-questionable. Every spring, without fail, he comes out to bring joy to those who love him. To be boiled alive, to have his shell peeled from his body and to be cooked in delicious gravys and sauces. For his friends he gives his life — I am too choked . . . I can say no more.

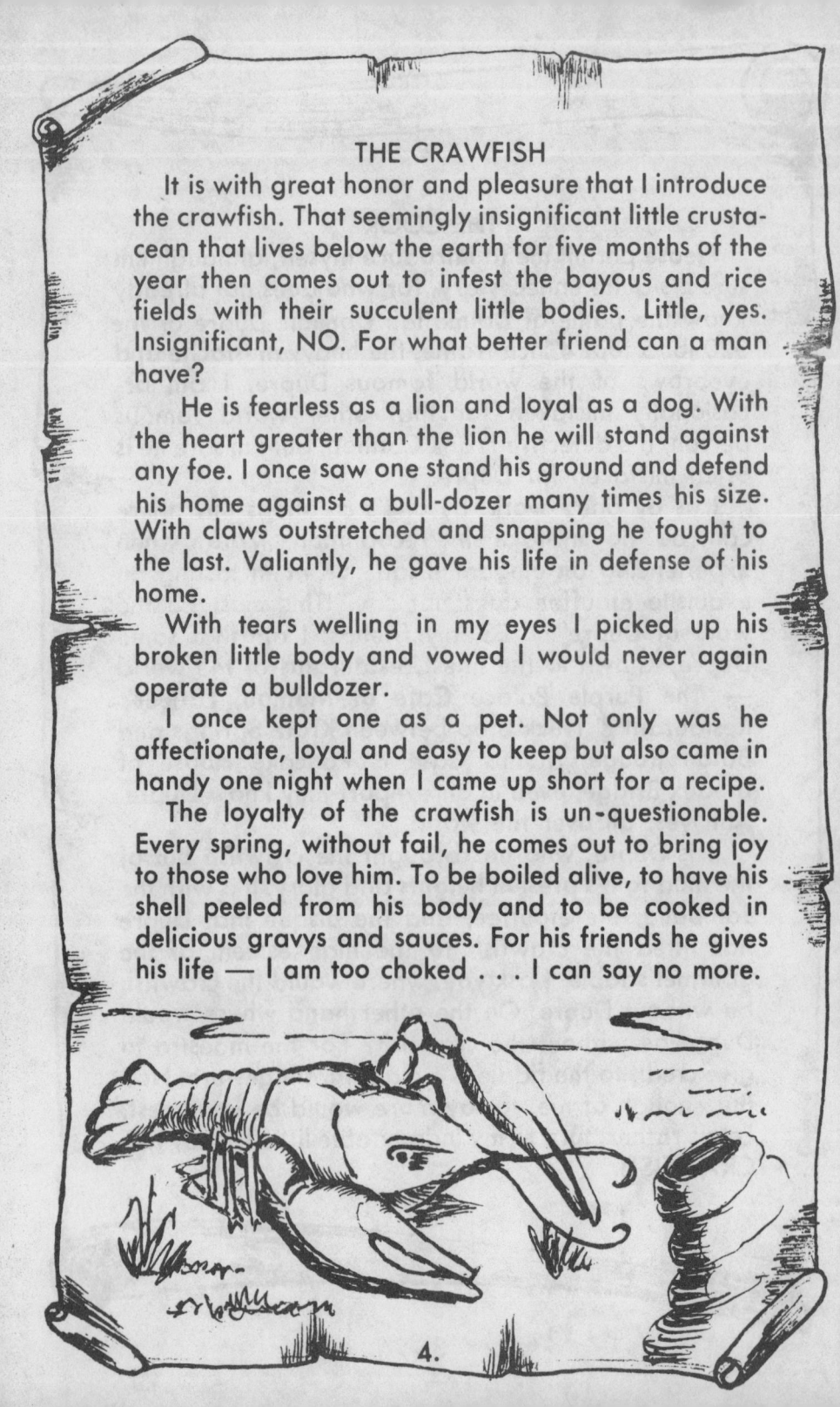

THINGS TO KNOW

1. Crawfish turn dark when cooked in a black iron pot. While this in no way detracts from the taste, it doesn't look as appetising as the beautiful pink color of crawfish cooked in a heavy aluminum skillet. Therefore, when a 'heavy pot or skillet' is mentioned, it is always to be of aluminum.

2. Many recipes call for a tablespoon of lemon juice. This is to cut the heavy odor and to tone down the strong taste. When doubling a recipe do not double the lemon juice, instead just add a few extra drops.

3. The term 'season to taste' will mean season with Tony Chachere's Famous Creole Seasoning. The combination of black and red pepper can make things a little hot so use your own judgment and taste on this point.

4. Many recipes call for onion, bell pepper, celery, garlic, onion tops and parsley and will be referred to as green seasonings. They are to be chopped fine before starting anything. Usually the onion tops and parsley are to be put aside to be added later as the onion tops melt to nothing and the parsley has a tendency to burn. Garlic is to be minced very fine and added with the bell pepper and other green seasonings.

THE ROUX

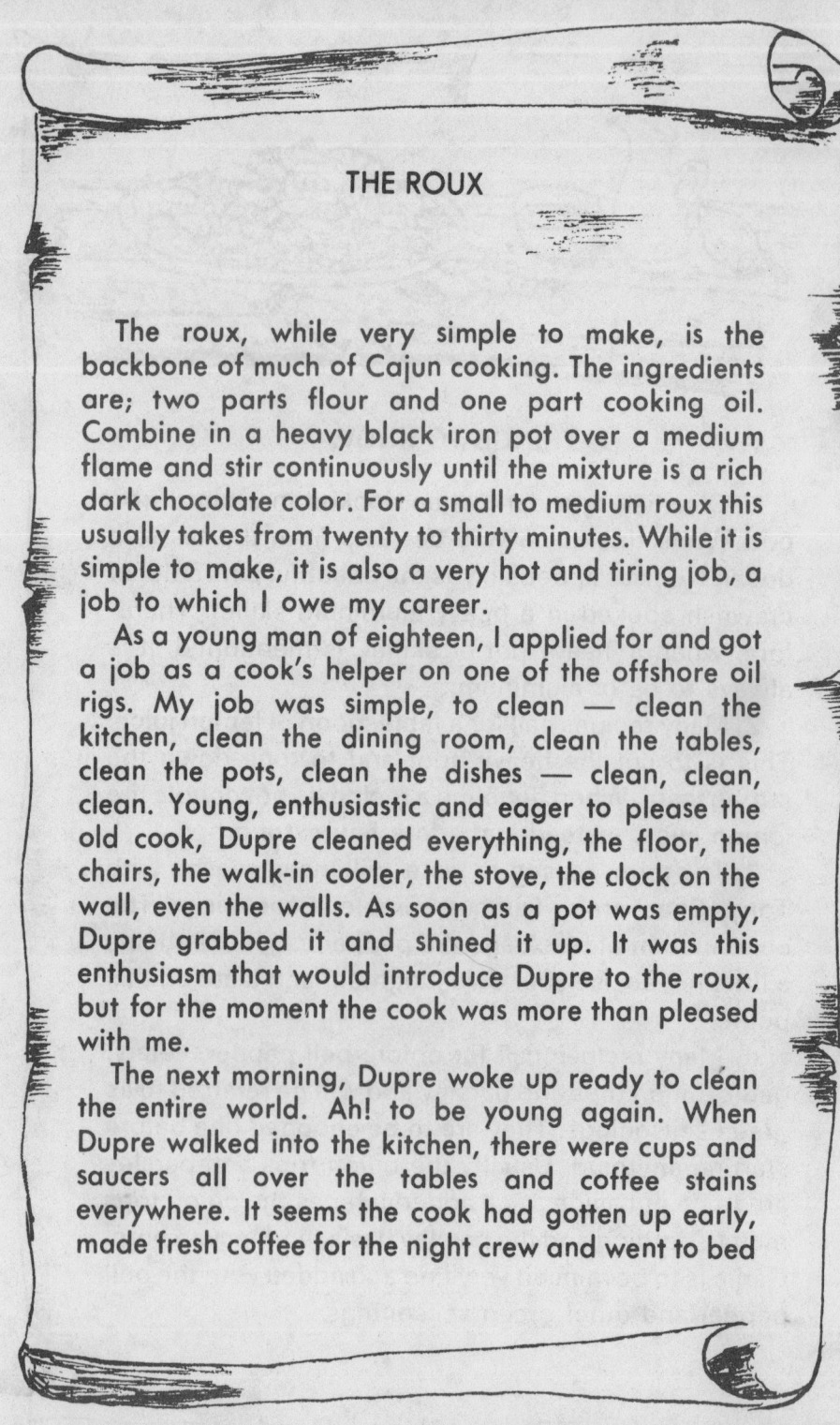

The roux, while very simple to make, is the backbone of much of Cajun cooking. The ingredients are; two parts flour and one part cooking oil. Combine in a heavy black iron pot over a medium flame and stir continuously until the mixture is a rich dark chocolate color. For a small to medium roux this usually takes from twenty to thirty minutes. While it is simple to make, it is also a very hot and tiring job, a job to which I owe my career.

As a young man of eighteen, I applied for and got a job as a cook's helper on one of the offshore oil rigs. My job was simple, to clean — clean the kitchen, clean the dining room, clean the tables, clean the pots, clean the dishes — clean, clean, clean. Young, enthusiastic and eager to please the old cook, Dupre cleaned everything, the floor, the chairs, the walk-in cooler, the stove, the clock on the wall, even the walls. As soon as a pot was empty, Dupre grabbed it and shined it up. It was this enthusiasm that would introduce Dupre to the roux, but for the moment the cook was more than pleased with me.

The next morning, Dupre woke up ready to clean the entire world. Ah! to be young again. When Dupre walked into the kitchen, there were cups and saucers all over the tables and coffee stains everywhere. It seems the cook had gotten up early, made fresh coffee for the night crew and went to bed for a little nap before fixing breakfast. Dupre decided to clean up 'spick and span' before the cook got back. I cleaned up everything, filled the sugar bowls and made a fresh pot of coffee. Everything was just right, everything shining, everything — except one thing.

On the stove was a huge black iron skillet as dirty as a sludge pit. In the bottom was about two inches of the nastiest brown mess I ever saw. Naturally Dupre went right to work on it.

When the cook woke up and came into the kitchen, the first thing he did was ask the whereabouts of his roux.

Dupre said, "I don't know, I haven't seen it."

"Are you sure?" the cook asked.

"All I've seen was a lot of dirty cups and saucers."

"Then where's the skillet that was on the stove?"

"The dirty one?" Dupre asked.

"The one with the roux in it." the cook said.

"What's that roux look like?" I asked.

The cook grabbed his hair and started pulling. I thought he was going to pull them all out. I also thought he was going to fire Dupre, but he was a compassionate man. Instead, he let me make him another roux. As a matter of fact, Dupre made five rouxs. The first four he burned. Very easy to burn a roux.

It took Dupre all day to make that roux — stirring and sweating, stirring and sweating, stirring and sweating. After he made the perfect roux Dupre still had all those dishes to do. Instead of being discouraged, Dupre was inspired — two days out and already a master cook.

When anyone asks me how I got my start I always say "With a roux."

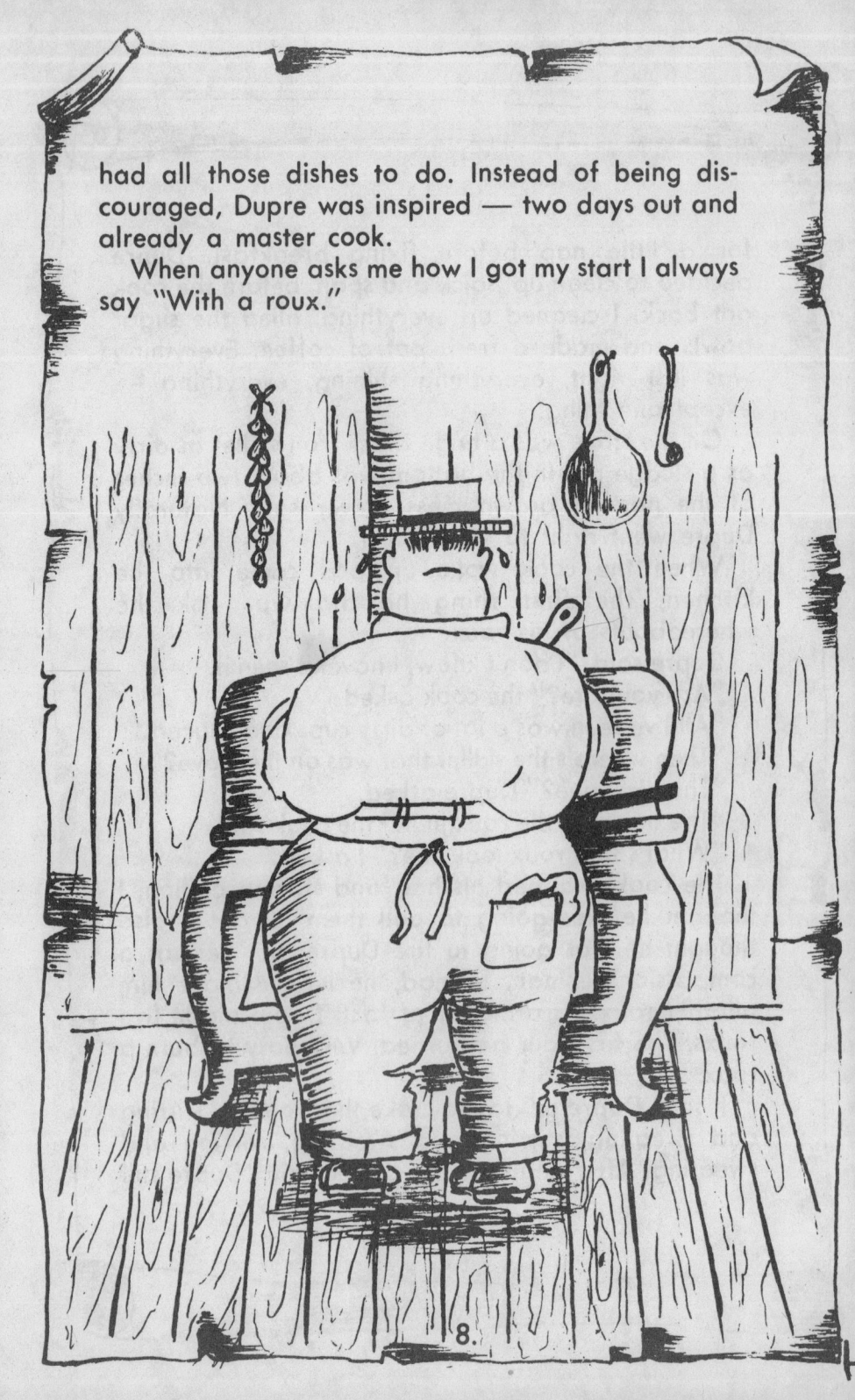

THE BOIL

20 lbs. live crawfish
1 bottle red pepper
6 onions (quartered)
3 whole pods garlic
4 dried bay leaves
1 tablespoon of dill
1 box salt
3 lemons (quartered)
1 tablespoon of mustard seeds
1 tablespoon of allspice

In a very large pot bring to a boil about one and one half gallons of water. Add all ingredients, except crawfish, and let boil about 5 minutes then add about half of the crawfish and boil for 10 to 15 minutes.

Remove crawfish to table covered with newspaper. Add the rest of the crawfish to boiling water and finish boiling. Peel and eat with crackers and a sauce made up of catsup, lemon juice, and a dash of Tobasco.

Serves 4 to 6 large men or one Dupre.

THE GUMBO

1 lb. crawfish (with fat)
1 bell pepper
1 onion
1 clove garlic
3 tablespoons roux
1 teaspoon bay leaf
1 qt. water or a little more
Seasoning to taste

Melt roux in heavy pot and add chopped onion, bell pepper and garlic to saute. (about five minutes). Add bay leaf and water and simmer for 2 hours. Add crawfish, crawfish fat and seasonings and cook for another hour. Serve in large soup bowls over cooked rice. Makes 4 servings.

This recipe may be changed up a little by adding a small can of tomato sauce immediately after sauteing the green seasonings.

THE BISQUE

For many years this recipe remained exclusively the property of Dupre. It was mine alone because I protected it like a mother hen defending her chick.

From all sides Dupre was besieged, everyone wanted this recipe. Flattery was attempted, bribery, threats, black-mail, even thievery was attempted, but to no avail. Dupre was too smart for that, he had made up the recipe 'out of his head' and that's where he kept it. Nothing could make me succumb — after all, Dupre is a man of character.

However, there was a widow who was persistent beyond belief, and as she was still a very beautiful woman, possessing ample assets, I was always polite.

One afternoon she stopped by my house, "Just to see what's cooking," she said. We had a little wine and talked food and in a short while the subject of my bisque recipe came up. She importuned — I smiled, she cajoled — I resisted, she pleaded — I prevailed, she begged — I stood fast, she offered her body — I gave her the recipe. Some women are extremely devious.

Since it is no longer a secret, I offer it to the world.

STUFFING FOR HEADS

1 lb. crawfish (with fat)
1 bell pepper
onion tops & parsley
1½ cup bread cubes
2 tablespoons butter
seasonings to taste

1 onion
1 clove garlic
2 stems celery
2 eggs
24 clean crawfish heads

Chop fine onions, bell pepper, garlic, celery and saute in butter. Chop crawfish coarse and add to green seasonings. Cut off fire then add bread cubes, onion tops, parsley, fat and eggs and blend into mixture. Stuff heads with this mixture then roll in flour and fry in deep fat at 350 degrees. Heads are done when they float to top of grease. Put aside until later.

SAUCE

1 lb. crawfish (with fat)
1 tablespoon lemon juice
1 clove garlic
1 tablespoon sugar
4 tablespoons roux
Tabasco
seasonings to taste
1 onion
1 stick celery
2 tablespoons butter
1 can tomato paste
onion tops & parsley
Worcestershire

Chop green seasonings and saute in butter then add crawfish, and lemon juice and saute about 5 minutes. Add 1 cup water and melt in roux then add tomato paste, onion tops, parsley, sugar, crawfish fat and season to taste. Add about a quart of water and simmer for about an hour and a half, adding water if necessary. Add stuffed crawfish heads and cook another 45 minutes.

Serve over cooked rice in bowls.

THE ETTOUFFEE

1 lb. crawfish
  (with fat)
1 tablespoon lemon juice
2 tablespoons green onions
1/2 cup red wine
seasonings to taste

1 large onion
1 bell pepper
1 stick butter
1 pod garlic
2 tablespoons roux
Tobasco

Chop bell pepper, onion, garlic and onion tops fine. Brown butter in heavy pot, add chopped green seasonings (except onion tops) and saute until wilted. Lower flame, add 3 cups water, roux and cover. Let simmer for about 1 hour then add crawfish, red wine and fat and cook 20 minutes more.

Serve over cooked rice with a fresh spinich salad topped with crisp bacon bits, croutons and salad oil.

The etouffee is one of the richest meals but one of the least fattening. I have, over a life time, consumed three or four tons of it and only 320 lbs. have stuck to my boans. You may eat as much of it as you like without fear of gaining a pound.

THE JAMBALAYA

1 lb. crawfish (with fat)
1 tablespoon lemon juice
1 small onion
1 bell pepper
1 clove garlic
2 stems celery
Onion tops and parsley
1 cup rice
1 can whole tomatoes
Butter
Seasonings to taste

Chop all green seasonings and saute in butter. Wash rice thoroughly and add raw to green seasonings along with tomatoes, onion tops, parsley and a little water. Cook about 40 minutes then add crawfish, lemon juice, fat and season to taste. Cook for another 20 minutes. Makes enough for 6.

A toss salad, hot rolls with an old-fashion apple betty for desert will compliment this dish nicely.

COURTBOUILLION

1 lb. crawfish (with fat)
1 bell pepper
3 stems celery
1 bay leaf
Worcestershire
dash of thyme
butter
1 tablespoon lemon juice
1 clove garlic
onion tops & parsley
1½ can tomato sauce
1 cup water
flour
seasonings to taste

Chop onion, bell pepper, garlic and celery and saute in large pot. Season crawfish to taste and add to pot with lemon juice. Saute another 5 minutes. Add other ingredients (including fat) and cook slowly for about one hour. Add one or two tablespoons flour to thicken. Season to taste.

Delicious served with buttered French peas and sliced tomatoes with a dill dressing.

STUFFED EGG PLANT

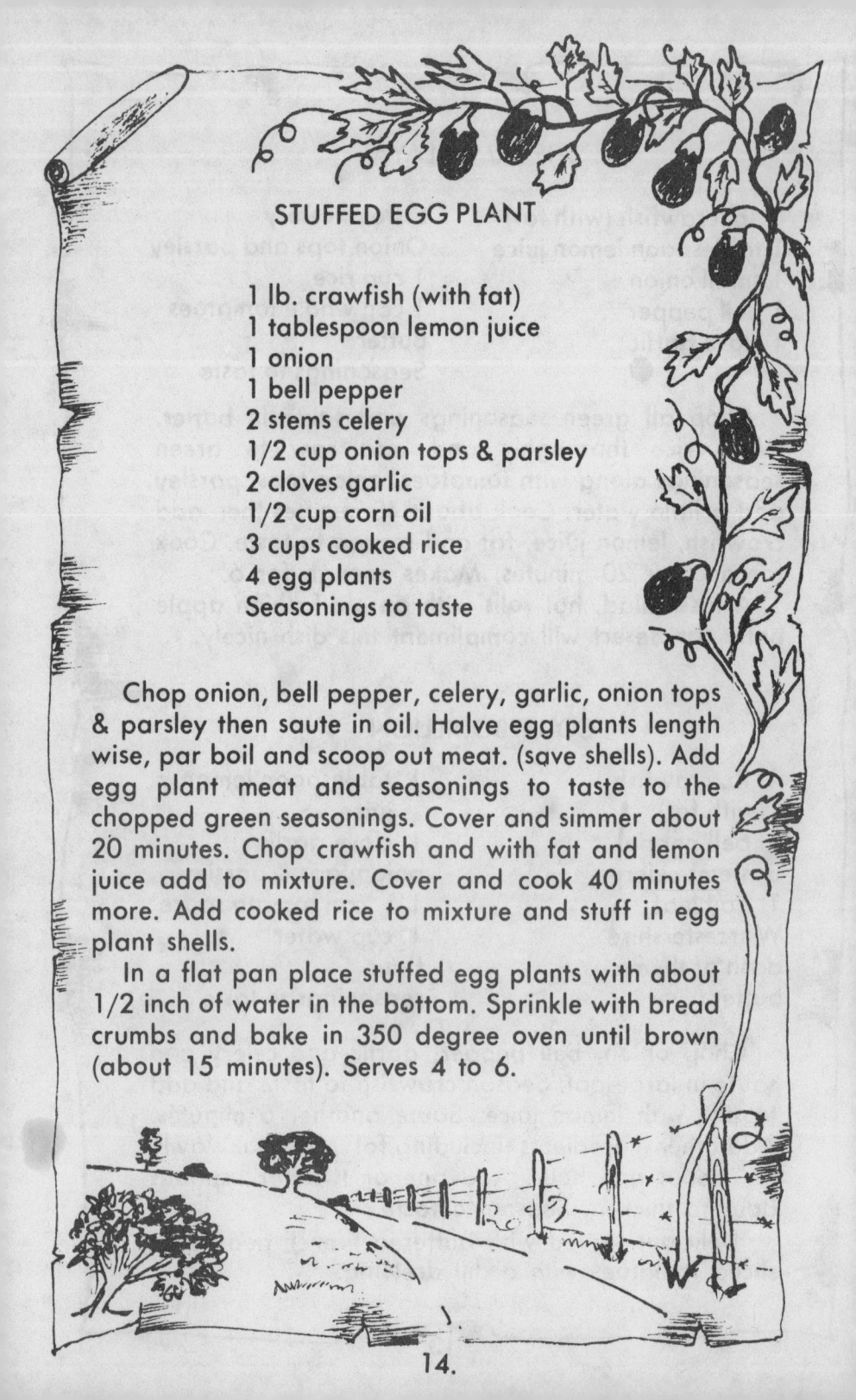

1 lb. crawfish (with fat)
1 tablespoon lemon juice
1 onion
1 bell pepper
2 stems celery
1/2 cup onion tops & parsley
2 cloves garlic
1/2 cup corn oil
3 cups cooked rice
4 egg plants
Seasonings to taste

Chop onion, bell pepper, celery, garlic, onion tops & parsley then saute in oil. Halve egg plants length wise, par boil and scoop out meat. (save shells). Add egg plant meat and seasonings to taste to the chopped green seasonings. Cover and simmer about 20 minutes. Chop crawfish and with fat and lemon juice add to mixture. Cover and cook 40 minutes more. Add cooked rice to mixture and stuff in egg plant shells.

In a flat pan place stuffed egg plants with about 1/2 inch of water in the bottom. Sprinkle with bread crumbs and bake in 350 degree oven until brown (about 15 minutes). Serves 4 to 6.

SMOTHERED

- 1 lb crawfish (with fat)
- 2 hot peppers
- 1 stick butter
- onion tops & parsley
- 2 tablespoons sherry
- 1 onion
- 1 bell pepper
- 1 stem celery
- 1 can of stewed tomatoes
- salt

Saute onions, bell pepper, and celery until wilted stirring constantly then add crawfish and saute 5 minutes. Add stewed tomatoes and chopped hot peppers and cook another 10 minutes then add crawfish fat, lemon juice, onion tops and parsley, sherry, seasonings to taste and cover. Simmer for twenty minutes.

Serve over cooked rice. Delicious with plain boiled potatoes with parsley butter and a large saucer of asparagus.

THE OKRA CASSEROLE

- 1 lb. dressed crawfish
- 1 tablespoon lemon juice
- 1 onion
- 1 small bell pepper
- 1 clove garlic
- 1 can whole tomatoes
- 1½ lbs. okra (cut in flat rounds)
- bread crumbs
- butter
- Seasonings to taste

Break up tomatoes and mix in chopped onion, bell pepper and garlic. Saute crawfish in butter and lemon juice for about 5 min. Chop okra into thin rounds and in a large casserole dish put a layer of okra at the bottom then a layer of crawfish over the okra. Over this pour the tomato mixture. Make another layer starting with the okra and continue until all ingredients are used up.

Bake at 350 degrees for about one hour. Top with bread crumbs about 10 minutes before done.

STUFFED TAILS

1 lb. crawfish
1 onion
1 bell pepper
2 eggs
Butter

1 tablespoon lemon juice
1 clove garlic
1 cup bread crumbs
Seasonings to taste

Saute about a dozen crawfish tails in butter and set aside. Finely chop onion, bell pepper, garlic and remaining crawfish. Add to this raw eggs, lemon juice, bread crumbs and season to taste. Make a heavy plyable paste by adding either bread crumbs or a little water. Around the crawfish tails that you have sauted, make balls of this mixture. Roll in flour and drop in deep fat (about 350 degrees) and cook until they float to the surface.

Goes good as a side dish and any left over mixture can be rolled into balls and fried.

FRIED CRAWFISH

1 lb. crawfish
1 tablespoon lemon juice
1/2 cup evaporated milk
1 cup flour
2 eggs
1 tablespoon of Worcestershire
Seasonings to taste
oil for frying

In a bowl, make a mixture of eggs, milk, lemon juice, Worcestershire and seasonings to taste. Marinate crawfish in mixture. Drain crawfish and roll in flour. Fry crawfish in 400 degree oil until crawfish floats to the top. Serves 4.

THE PIQUANT

1 lb. crawfish (with fat)
1 tablespoon lemon juice
1/2 cup water
1/2 cup red wine
Tobasco
Seasonings to taste

1 onion
1 bell pepper
1 stem celery
1 clove garlic
1 16-oz. can tomatoes
1 teaspoon soy sauce

Chop onion, bell pepper, celery, garlic and saute in butter. Add water and all other ingredients and season to taste. Cook over medium fire for one hour. Serve over cooked rice.

With this nothing more is needed but buttered French bread and cucumber salad.

THE STEW

1 lb. crawfish (with fat)
1 onion
1 bell pepper
3 tablespoons roux
1 can tomato paste
Seasonings to taste
1 tablespoon lemon juice
1 clove garlic
1 stem celery
Worcestershire
2 tablespoons white wine
Onion tops and parsley

Chop green seasonings fine and saute in heavy aluminum pot. Mix in roux, tomato paste and a little water and cook about 20 minutes over medium fire stirring constantly. Stir in a dash of Worcestershire and two tablespoons white wine then add crawfish, crawfish fat, onion tops and parsley and season to taste. Cover and simmer for about one hour.

Serve over cooked rice with a cucumber and onion salad along with hot French bread and butter. Serves 6.

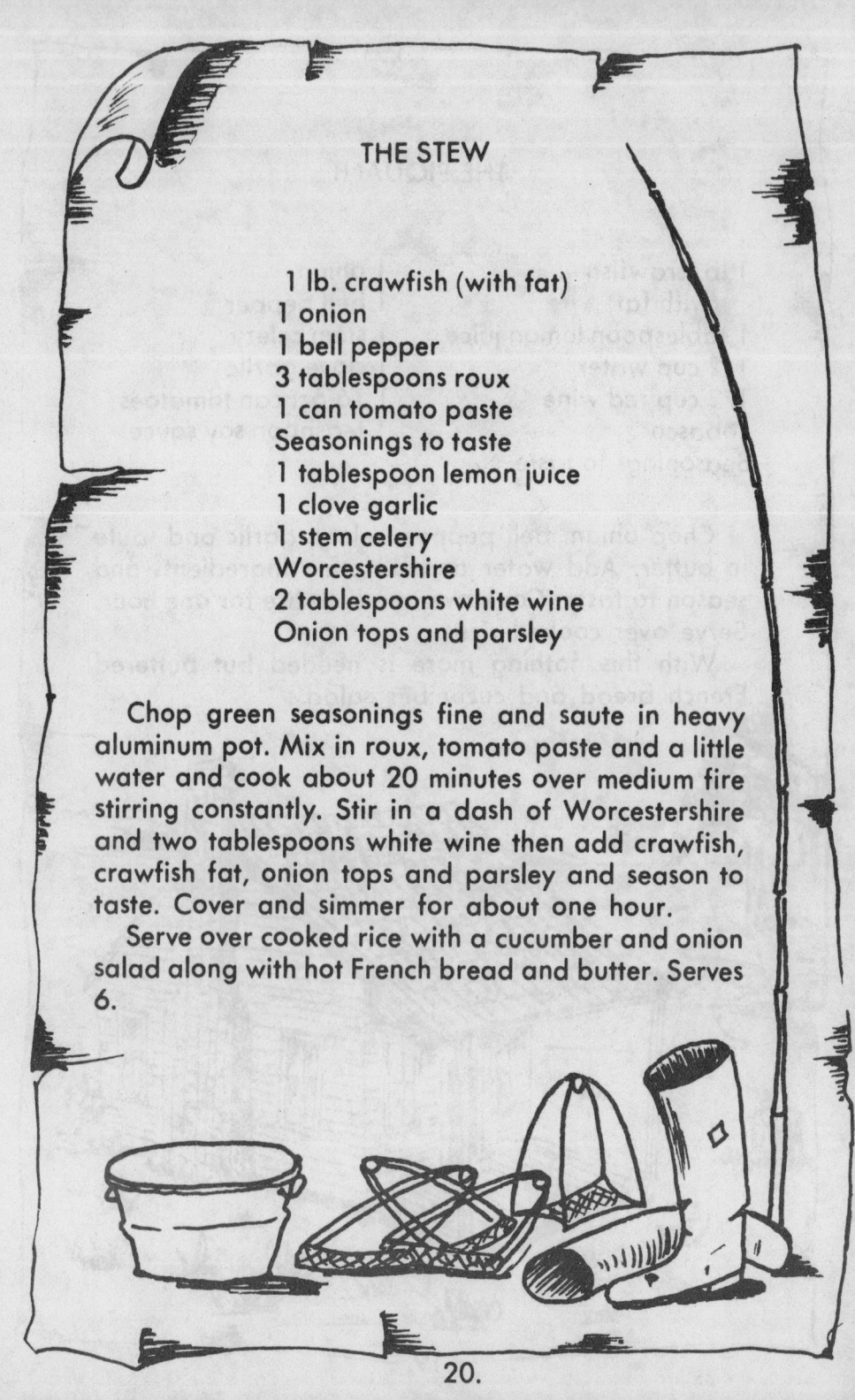

THE SUPREME

1 lb. crawfish (with fat)
1 tablespoon of lemon juice
1 small can of tomatoes
seasonings to taste

1 onion
1 bellpepper
1 clove garlic
butter
dash of basil
Worchestershire

Chop onions, bell peppers and garlic fine and saute in butter. Add tomatoes, basil and seasonings to taste then cover and simmer 10 minutes. Add crawfish, crawfish fat and lemon juice and cook 20 to 30 minutes over medium heat covered. Serves 4.

A celery salad with mustard dressing and some good old fashion corn bread is a must with this recipe. Maybe a chilled bottle of dry red wine to wash it down.

THE SALAD

1/2 lb. dressed crawfish
1 carrot
4 raddish
2 hard boiled eggs
Thousand Island dressing

4 tomatoes
1 cucumber
Lettuce
Parsley
Seasonings to taste

Boil crawfish and season to taste. Cut the tops out of tomatoes and serrate top edge into about six points. Place lettuce leaves on 4 saucers then the tomatoes on the lettuce. Fill tomatoes with crawfish and around the tomatoes place sliced cucumbers curled carrots and sliced radish. Cover liberally with Thousand Island dressing and top with sliced eggs.

EGGPLANT CASSEROLE

1 lb. crawfish
   (with fat)
1 onion
1 clove garlic
1 egg
butter
parmesan cheese
1 tablespoon of
   white wine
1 tablespoon lemon
   juice
1 bell pepper
2 eggplants
bread crumbs
onion tops & parsley
seasonings to taste

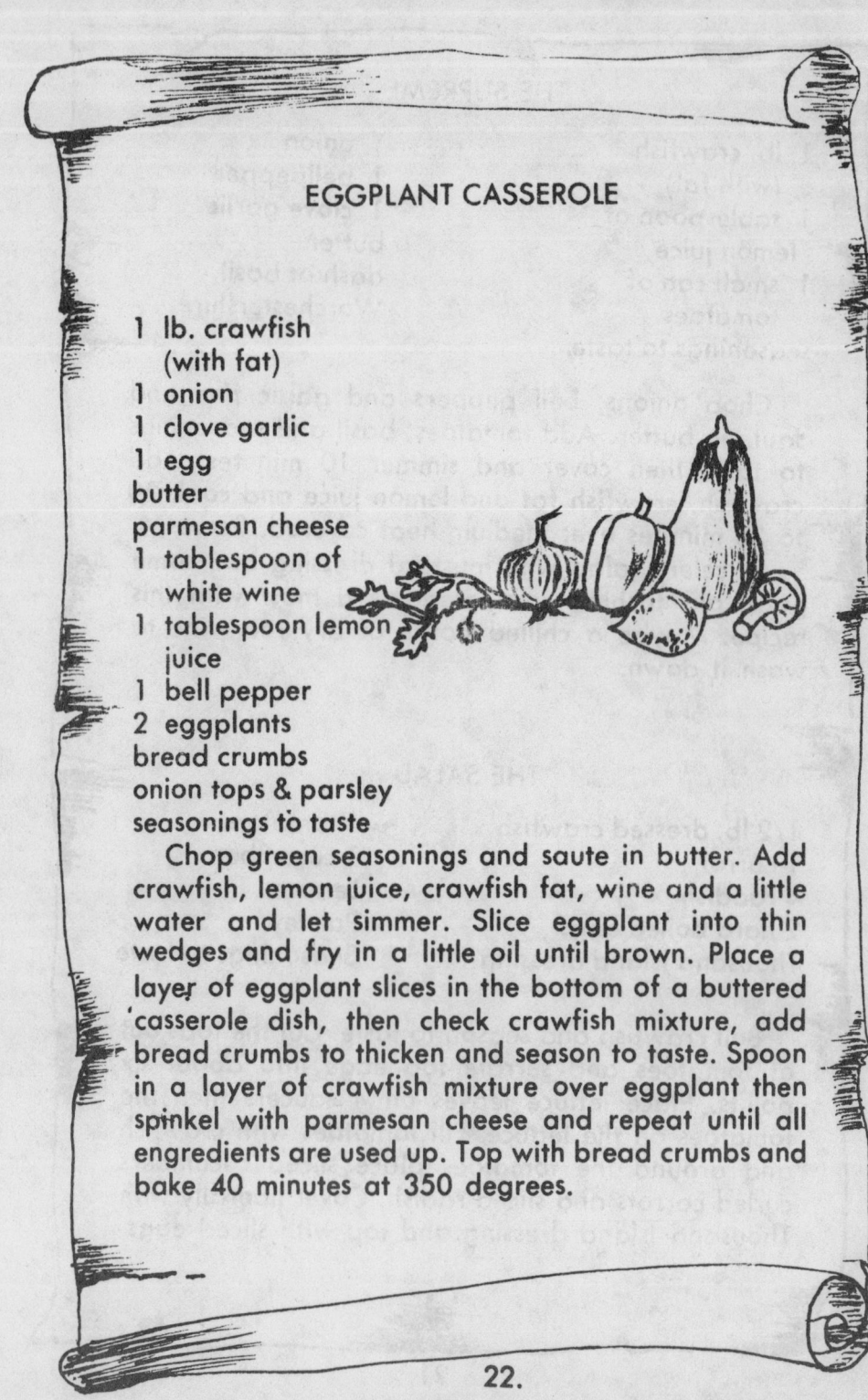

Chop green seasonings and saute in butter. Add crawfish, lemon juice, crawfish fat, wine and a little water and let simmer. Slice eggplant into thin wedges and fry in a little oil until brown. Place a layer of eggplant slices in the bottom of a buttered casserole dish, then check crawfish mixture, add bread crumbs to thicken and season to taste. Spoon in a layer of crawfish mixture over eggplant then spinkel with parmesan cheese and repeat until all engredients are used up. Top with bread crumbs and bake 40 minutes at 350 degrees.

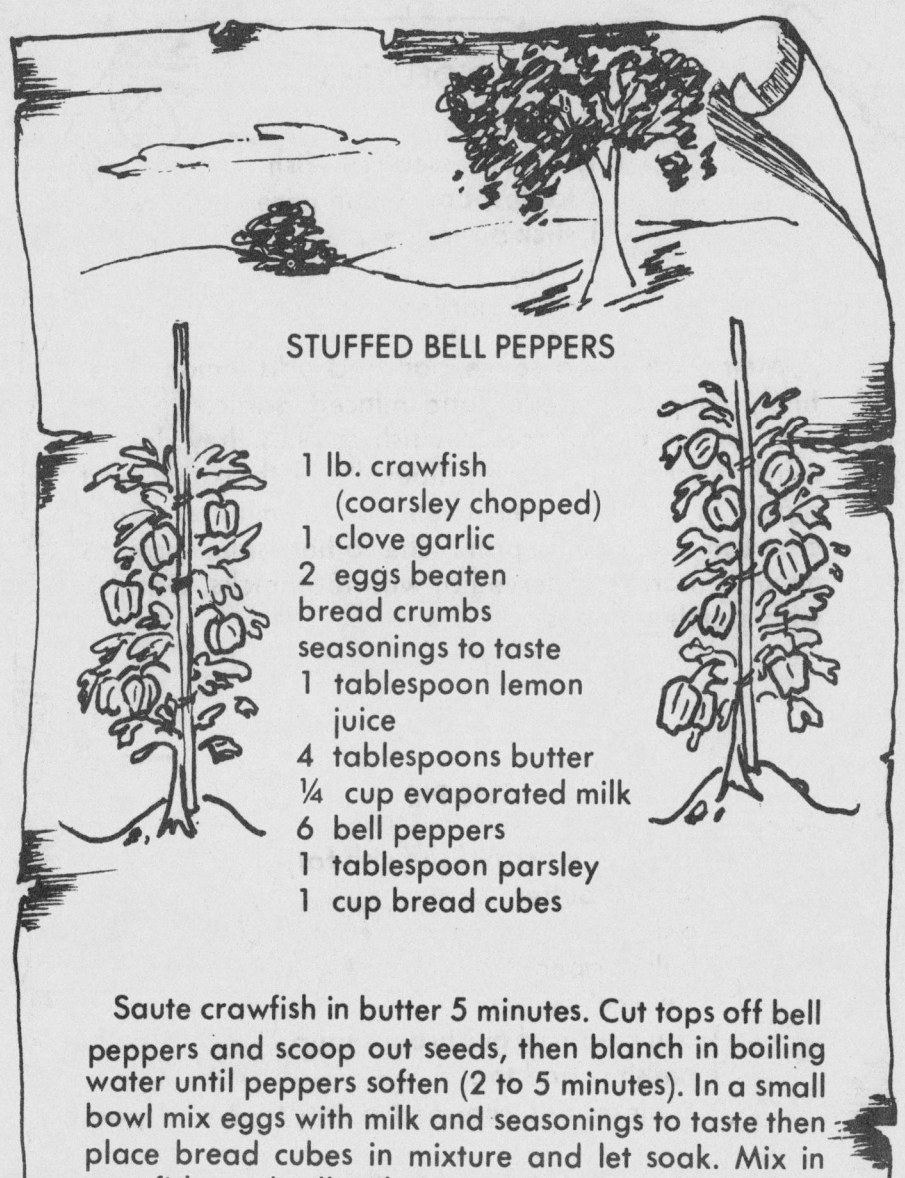

STUFFED BELL PEPPERS

1 lb. crawfish
   (coarsley chopped)
1 clove garlic
2 eggs beaten
bread crumbs
seasonings to taste
1 tablespoon lemon
   juice
4 tablespoons butter
¼ cup evaporated milk
6 bell peppers
1 tablespoon parsley
1 cup bread cubes

Saute crawfish in butter 5 minutes. Cut tops off bell peppers and scoop out seeds, then blanch in boiling water until peppers soften (2 to 5 minutes). In a small bowl mix eggs with milk and seasonings to taste then place bread cubes in mixture and let soak. Mix in crawfish and all other ingredients except bread crumbs. Add more bread cubes if mixture is too thin.

Stuff peppers with mixture and stand in pan with about ½ inch of water in the bottom. Mix 2 talespoons of melted butter with bread crumbs and sprinkle over top of each pepper. Bake in 350 degree oven until bread crumbs brown.

HORS D'OEUVRES

1/2 lb. dressed crawfish
1 tablespoon lemon juice
1 stick butter
Parsley
1 clove garlic

Melt butter in a sauce pan and add lemon juice, finely chopped parsley and minced garlic.

In a flat pan place crawfish so that they do not touch each other. Paint liberally with sauce and place in 350 degree oven for 3 minutes. Turn crawfish over and paint the other side. Broil 3 minutes more and serve hot with toothpicks. Garnish with parsley leaves.

THE PIE

1 lb. dressed crawfish (with fat)
3/4 stick butter
1 onion
1 bell pepper
1 stem celery
1 can cream of mushroom soup
1 pie shell and top
2 tablespoons chopped onion tops and parsley

Chop green seasonings fine. Brown butter in heavy skillet and add chopped seasonings to saute. Add crawfish, crawfish fat, mushroom soup and a little water to mixture. Cover and simmer 20 minutes. Next add onion tops and parsly and cook another 10 minutes. Place in pie shell and cover with top. Bake at 300 degrees until pie crust is brown. Makes 4 servings.

BIENVILLE

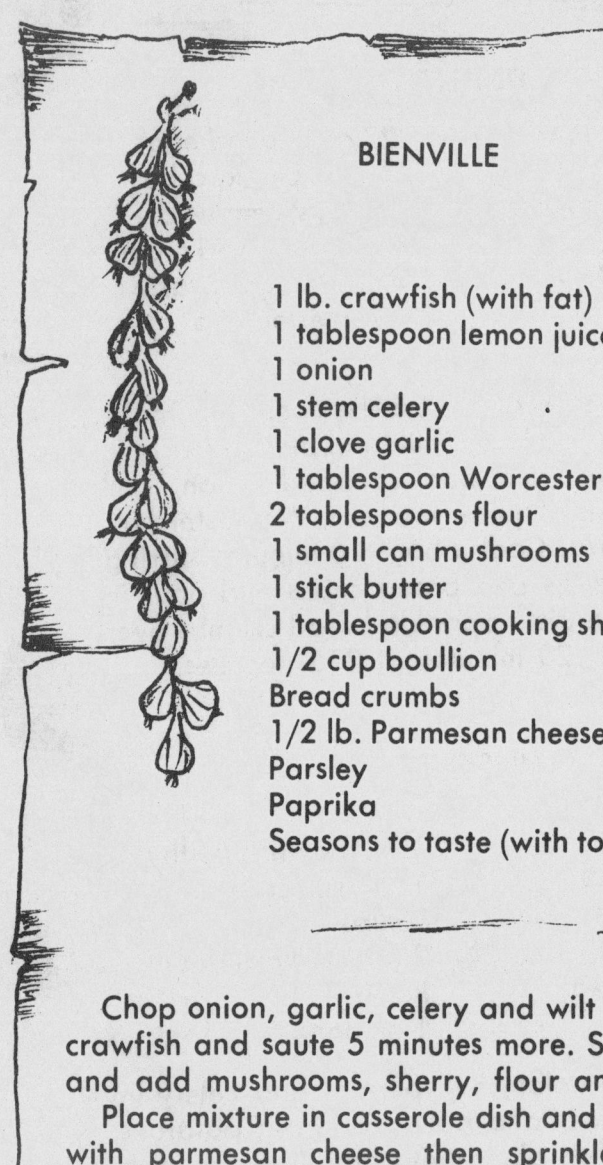

1 lb. crawfish (with fat)
1 tablespoon lemon juice
1 onion
1 stem celery
1 clove garlic
1 tablespoon Worcestershire
2 tablespoons flour
1 small can mushrooms
1 stick butter
1 tablespoon cooking sherry
1/2 cup boullion
Bread crumbs
1/2 lb. Parmesan cheese
Parsley
Paprika
Seasons to taste (with tobasco)

Chop onion, garlic, celery and wilt in butter. Add crawfish and saute 5 minutes more. Season to taste and add mushrooms, sherry, flour and boullion.
Place mixture in casserole dish and cover liberally with parmesan cheese then sprinkle with bread crumbs and paprika. Bake at 375 degrees for 10 to 15 minutes or until bread crumbs brown. Serve with baked potato and toss salad.

DEVILED

1 lb. crawfish (with fat)
1 tablespoon lemon juice
1/2 onion
1 clove garlic
1/2 bell pepper
Tobasco
2 hard boiled eggs
2 cups bread cubes (crust removed)
1/2 cup bread crumbs
Seasonings to taste
Worcestershire

Using a little butter and 2 tablespoons flour make a smooth paste. Add 1 cup milk and blend over low heat until smooth then add chopped onion, bell pepper, garlic, lemon juice, tobasco, Worcestershire and crawfish w/fat. Cook about 10 minutes stirring constantly. Add eggs and bread cubes and pour in buttered casserole dish. Sprinkle bread crumbs over the top and bake 20 minutes at 375 degrees.

THE SOUP

1 bell pepper
1 bay leaf
2 potatoes
Butter
Seasonings to taste
Paprika
1 lb. crawfish (with fat)
1 stem celery
2 cups milk
2 tablespoons flour
Parsley
1 onion

Saute crawfish, onion, bell pepper and celery in butter. Dice potatoes and par boil. Drain potatoes and add to crawfish along with bay leaf, crawfish fat and about a cup of water. Season to taste and simmer about 10 minutes then remove from heat.

Make a smooth paste by slowly mixing 1/2 cup milk to 2 cups flour, stirring constantly to eliminate all lumps. Add mixture to crawfish and bring to a boil stirring constantly. Add remaining milk and simmer a few minutes. Garnish with paprika and finely chopped parsley.

THE FONDUE

1 lb. crawfish
2 cups bread cubes
2 cups milk
3 eggs

1 tablespoon lemon juice
2 cups grated cheese
1 stick butter
Seasonings to taste

Saute crawfish in butter and lemon juice for about 5 minutes. In a casserole dish arrange in layers; bread cubes, crawfish, and cheese. Lightly beat eggs and combine with milk and seasonings to taste. Pour mixture over contents in casserole and set casserole in hot water. Bake at 350 degrees for about one hour. Serves 6.

THE AU GRATIN

1 lb. crawfish (with fat)
1 tablespoon lemon juice
2 tablespoons butter
Tobasco

2 tablespoons sherry
1/2 cup heavy cream
Parmesan cheese
Bread crumbs
Seasonings to taste

Saute crawfish in butter and lemon juice for 5 minutes. Season to taste and place in shallow casserole dish along with crawfish fat and a dash of tobasco. Add sherry and heavy cream blended with 3 tablespoons of Parmesan cheese. Sprinkle top with bread crumbs and add extra graded parmesan. Cook in 375 degree oven for 20 minutes.

Serve with noodles and a salad of peas and slivered green onions topped with an olive oil dressing.

CONGEALED SALAD

1 lb. crawfish (without fat)
1 tablespoon lemon juice
1 onion
1 bell pepper
2 stems celery
2 green onions
1 clove garlic
Parsley
2 envelopes gelatin
1 small can tomato sauce
1 cup tomato juice
Tobasco
Prepared Horse Raddish
Worcestershire
Seasonings to taste

Season crawfish to taste and boil in water and lemon juice for about 15 minutes then drain. In 1/2 cup water disolve gelatin thoroughly. Chop green seasonings and mix with boiled crawfish. Pour tomato juice and tomato sauce in a sauce pan and heat then add to gelatin and stir well. Add crawfish and vegetable mixture to gelatin and pour into buttered mold. Be sure no lemon juice gets into this mixture as the gelatin will not congeal. Chill and serve.

THE CREOLE

1 lb. crawfish (with fat)
1 onion
1 clove garlic
1 large can tomatoes
Butter
Seasons to taste
1 tablespoon lemon juice
1 bell pepper
Onion tops & parsley
2 tablespoons roux
2 tablespoons red wine

    Saute chopped onion, bell pepper, and garlic in butter. Add roux and stir well. Stir in crawfish and season to taste. Add tomatoes, lemon juice, fat and wine and simmer in covered pot for 40 minutes adding a little water if necessary. Add onion tops and parsley about 20 minutes before done. Serve over cooked rice.

    Delicious with a cucumber salad, French bread and sliced apples and oranges with grapes.

MUSHROOM CASSEROLE

1 lb. crawfish
1 large can mushrooms
8 hard boiled eggs
1/4 cup butter
2 cups milk
1/4 cup flour
1½ cup grated cheese
Seasonings to taste
Bread crumbs

    Place a layer of mushrooms in the bottom of a large casserole dish. Chop and mash eggs with a fork and mix with raw crawfish seasoned to taste. Place a layer of this mixture over the mushrooms. Make a white sauce of butter, flour and milk. Stir in one cup grated cheese and cook over low heat until choose melts. Pour over mushrooms and crawfish and cover with remaining cheese. Sprinkle top with bread crumbs and bake for about 40 minutes at 350 degrees.

THE AMANDINE

1/4 cup lemon juice
1 clove garlic
1/4 cup olive oil
Worcestershire
2 tablespoons vermouth
Seasonings to taste

1 lb. crawfish
1/2 small onion
Tobasco
1/2 cup blanched slivered almonds
Butter

Make a marinade of olive oil, lemon juice and a dash of Worcestershire. Place crawfish in marinade and let stand one or two hours. Remove crawfish and saute in butter along with chopped onions and garlic for about five minutes. Add marinade, Tobasco and vermouth and simmer five minutes. Cut off heat and add almonds. Serve over cooked rice.

BAR-B-Q STUFFED CRAWFISH

3 doz. large crawfish tails
1/4 stem celery
1 cup cooked crab meat
1/2 cup milk
Butter
1/4 onion

1 clove garlic
1/2 cup bread crumbs
Worcestershire
Tobasco
Seasonings to taste

Chop and saute onion, celery and garlic in butter. Cut off fire and add crab meat, bread crumbs, Worcestershire, Tobasco and season to taste. Add milk a little at a time stirring constantly to get desired thickness. Make balls of this mixture around crawfish tails. Roll in flour and chill. When ready to cook place in pan and broil or Bar-B-Q in closed pit. Baste with prepared Bar-B-Q sauce or your favorite home made. Makes a delicious side dish or hors d'oeuvre.

THE CAJUN

While the Cajun has as many facets as a hand full of diamonds, there is one aspect that is appropriate to a cook book — his love for food . . . any food.

I often say to myself, "Dupre, I'm sure glad you were born a Cajun. Think of all the good dishes you would have missed."

There is a story told of a mother crawfish who took her brood of children out for a walk and to teach them something of life. When they approached a horse she told them not to worry because a horse only eats grass or hay. A bit further, they came upon a chicken and she told them not to be afraid because a chicken only eats corn and chicken feed. Further on up the 'road of life' the mother crawfish began to scream in panic "Run for your life! Run for your life! That's a Cajun — he eats anything!! I've had a recent experience that bears this out and I would like to relate it to you.

I was visiting a friend who owns a small farm and who raises almost every kind of poultry and foul. In his barnyard you'll see ducks, geese, turkeys, pidgeons, doves, pheasants, quail and chickens he keeps. On this particular day we were in the kitchen cooking one of may favorit dishes, guineas gumbo, when he asked me to accompany him outside as he wanted to show me a new acquisition. I was never more surprised.

Among the more common birds of his menagerie strutted two of the most beautiful peacocks I've ever seen. The male was in full plumage with a tail that could only be called magnificent.

I commented on the exceptional beauty of the birds and on the regal way they moved about the yard. My friend seemed unimpressed but mentioned that he couldn't wait for the hen to start setting. When I asked why he said "I've never tasted a peacock before."

I was appalled at this attitude but decided to hold my peace. After all they were his peacocks and besides that I myself had never tasted a peacock.

The secret is in the seasoning

The secret to good cooking is in the seasoning... and Tony Chachere's Famous Creole Seasoning now unlocks the secret to truly unique eating experiences. Tony put the recipes in his Cajun Country Cookbook, and now it's available in an 8 ounce carton at your supermarket.

Tony's seasoning contains all the ingredients that make Creole cooking so delicious.

For Product, Price and Ordering information call:
(318) 948-4691 or Toll Free 1-800-551-9066.

VISA or MASTERCARD Accepted.

Write: **CREOLE FOODS**
P.O. Box 1687
Opelousas, La. 70570

0 71998 00060 0